Letter to My Mom
My Thoughts, My Questions, & My Feelings

Guy C. Jeanty, Ph.D.

JEANTY COUNSELING
& CONSULTING
WHEN YOU NEED A HAND, HELP IS AVAILABLE

Published by Jeanty Counseling & Consulting, LLC in 2017
First edition; First printing
©2017 Guy C. Jeanty
www.drjeanty.com
www.emotions101.net

Publisher's Note

To my mom, Cesarine Jeanty, who gave me the greatest gift of all, LOVE. From my earliest recollection, I have always known that I was loved. Thank you.

Letter to My Mom

At times you may have very important things you want to say or important questions that you would like to ask. Trying to let another person know how you feel can be very difficult, and finding the words to express yourself how you feel can be even more difficult. Perhaps the other person may not be a very good listener, or maybe you get interrupted when you try to say how you feel. Maybe you are being told how you should feel and what you should think. Writing a letter can be a very good way to express how you feel, even if you choose not to share the letter with anyone. Writing a letter can make you feel better because it gives you a chance to express how you feel. Knowing how you feel and expressing your feelings are important parts of solving a problem. Find a quiet and private place and begin writing your letter. In the journal section, additional thoughts, feelings and or experiences can be written.

A Note to Caregivers

If you are a caregiver (such as a parent, relative, or guardian) or a professional person, children should be given the opportunity to decide whether or not they want to write the letter and some degree of privacy should be granted depending on the age and unique circumstances of the child's life. This letter can also be used in conjunction with counseling.

Dear _____ :

I wonder _____

_____

_____

_____

_____

_____

_____

_____

_____

_____

_____

_____

_____

_____

_____

_____

Sometimes I think that _____

_____

_____

_____

_____

_____

_____

_____

_____

_____

_____

_____

_____

_____

_____

_____

_____

_____

_____

_____

_____

At times I feel _____

_____

_____

_____

_____

_____

_____

_____

_____

_____

_____

_____

_____

_____

_____

_____

_____

_____

I don't understand _____

_____

_____

_____

_____

_____

_____

_____

_____

_____

_____

_____

_____

_____

_____

_____

_____

_____

_____

I want to know why _____

_____

_____

_____

_____

_____

_____

_____

_____

_____

_____

_____

_____

_____

_____

_____

_____

_____

I want you to know that

I'm happiest when _____

_____

_____

_____

_____

_____

_____

_____

_____

_____

_____

_____

_____

_____

_____

_____

_____

_____

I wish that _____

_____

_____

_____

_____

_____

_____

_____

_____

_____

_____

_____

_____

_____

_____

_____

_____

_____

Sincerely yours,

Journal

Journal

Journal

Journal

Journal

Journal

Journal

Journal

Journal

Journal

www.ingramcontent.com/pod-product-compliance
Lightning Source LLC
LaVergne TN
LVHW072110070426
835509LV00002B/94